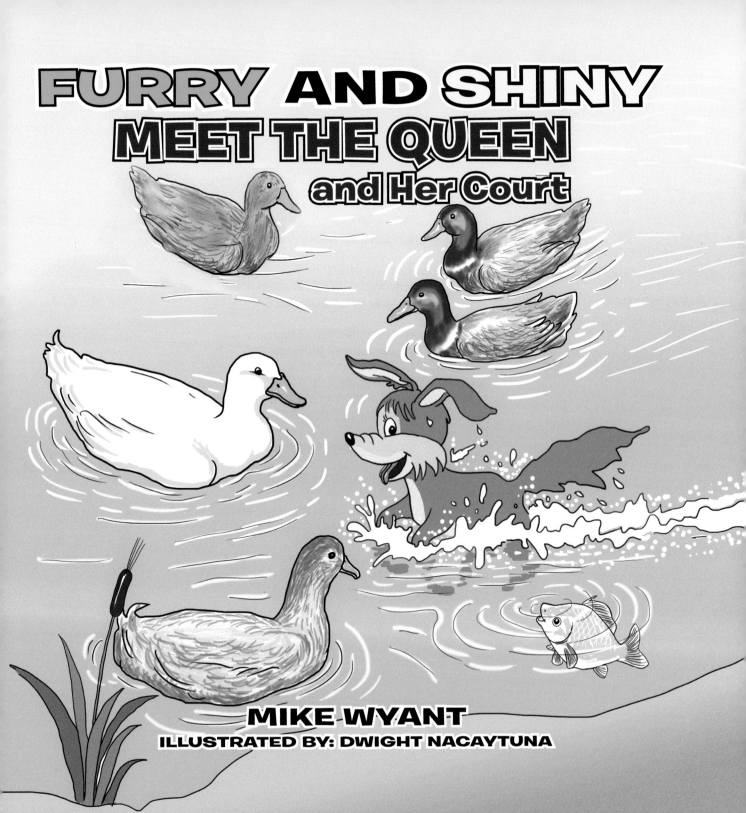

FURRY AND SHINY
MEET THE QUEEN
and Her Court

MIKE WYANT

ILLUSTRATED BY: DWIGHT NACAYTUNA

Print information available on the last page

Rev. date: 07/15/2015

To order additional copies of this book, contact:
Xlibris
1-888-795-4274
www.Xlibris.com
Orders@Xlibris.com

NOTE: Parents, the author has created a special bookmark which includes small portions of artificial fur on a picture of Furry and a shiny portion of material on a picture of Shiny. The child may feel these materials while the book is being read to them. However, if you feel the child might remove these materials and swallow them, please keep the book mark separate and under your control. For a copy of this bookmark, please send a #10 envelope, self addressed to you and including a stamp for mailing. Thank you, Mike Wyant.

203 Standard St., El Segundo, CA, 90245

It's a beautiful day on Crystal Lake with all the birds chirping in the bushes and the ducks on the lake.

Furry and Shiny are at the lake talking when they hear many loud squawks.

They look on the lake
and a short way off
is a large white Duck
with her friends.

4

The friends are two beautiful Mallard ducks and two brown ducks.

The other creatures at the lake call her the Queen and her court since she looks so stately.

But, today, there are only the Queen
and three ducks, one is missing!

7

The squawking gets louder and the ducks are all flapping their wings, jumping up and down in the water. "Help us, help us!" the ducks cry out.

One of the ducks flys over to Furry and Shiny for help.

A teenage boy has been fishing and accidently hooked one of the ducks on his fishing line.

The boy is laughing at the duck who is being dragged in to the shore.

"Please help us" said the Queen duck to Furry and Shiny.

So, Furry runs to where the boy is and barks at him several times while Furry shows his teeth.

The boy drops the fishing pole and runs away.

14

Furry jumps into the water and swims to the duck. "I'm here to help you!" Furry says.

Furry takes the line in his teeth and bites it in two, leaving the hook still in the duck.

Furry asks the duck, "Does it hurt now", but the duck says "No, not now, it's just stuck in my bill".

The Queen and the other members of her court fly over to where Furry and Shiny are and thank them for their help. "Thank you Furry and Shiny for your help!"

18

The Queen makes a promise that she and her friends will not go after the small fish any more. "We promise you we will not go after any more small fish again!

Furry jumps into the water again and paddles around playing with his and Shiny's new friends.

The sun sets on Crystal Lake.

Printed in the United States
By Bookmasters